Riches of the Earth

Apples

Irene Franck and David Brownstone

GROLIER

An imprint of Scholastic Library Publishing
Danbury, Connecticut

Credits and Acknowledgments

abbreviations: t (top), b (bottom), l (left), r (right), c (center)

Image credits: Agricultural Research Service Library: 1, 4, and 19 (Scott Bauer); 5, 8, and 21l (Keith Weller); 14 (Peggy Greb), 21r (Doug Wilson); Art Resource: 16t (Ricco/Maresca Gallery); Getty Images/PhotoDisc/PhotoLink: 7r (J. Luke), 11 (D. Falconer), 29; John Marshall: 9, 20, 22; National Aeronautics and Space Administration (NASA): 1t and running heads; Photo Researchers, Inc.: 7l (Hans Reinhard/Okapia); U.S. Apple Association: 3, 6, 12-13 (all), 16b, 24, 26, 27, 28; U.S. Department of Agriculture: 10 (Ken Hammond), 17 and 23 (Doug Wilson); Woodfin Camp & Associates: 15 (Lindsay Hebberd), 25 (Catherine Karnow). Original image drawn for this book by K & P Publishing Services: 18.

Our thanks to Joe Hollander, Phil Friedman, and Laurie McCurley at Scholastic Library Publishing; to photo researchers Susan Hormuth, Robin Sand, and Robert Melcak; to copy editor Michael Burke; and to the librarians throughout the northeastern library network, in particular to the staff of the Chappaqua Library—director Mark Hasskarl; the expert reference staff, including Martha Alcott, Michele J. Capozzella, Maryanne Eaton, Catherine Paulsen, Jane Peyraud, Paula Peyraud, and Carolyn Reznick; and the circulation staff, headed by Barbara Le Sauvage—for fulfilling our wide-ranging research needs.

Published 2003 by Grolier
Division of Scholastic Library Publishing
Old Sherman Turnpike
Danbury, Connecticut 06816

For information address the publisher:
Scholastic Library Publishing, Grolier Division
Old Sherman Turnpike, Danbury, Connecticut 06816

© 2003 Irene M. Franck and David M. Brownstone

Library of Congress Cataloging-in-Publication Data

Franck, Irene M.
    Apples / Irene Franck and David Brownstone.
      p. cm. -- (Riches of the earth ; v. 1)
    Summary: Provides information about apples and their importance in everyday life.
    Includes bibliographical references and index.
    ISBN 0-7172-5730-4 (set : alk. paper) -- ISBN 0-7172-5713-4 (vol. 1 : alk paper)
      1. Apples--Juvenile literature [1. Apples.] I. Brownstone, David M. II. Title.

SB363.F75 2003
641.3'411--dc21

2003044077

Printed in the United States of America

Designed by K & P Publishing Services

Contents

People often say that something is as "all-American as apple pie," because apples are so widespread and popular in the United States. But modern eating apples originally came from Eurasia and were brought to North America only in the early 1600s.

Tasty Apples

You've probably heard the phrase "as American as apple pie." Apples are certainly widely grown in the United States, and apple pie and many other apple products are widely made and eaten in North America. In fact, the average American eats more than 19 pounds of apples every year! However, the kind of apples we love came late to the Americas, arriving only with European colonists (see p. 13).

In many parts of Europe and Asia, apples have been grown and eaten for thousands of years. Indeed, people were eating apples long before they knew how to read and write. The apple was among the first fruits widely used by humans (see p. 12) and is still one of the most popular fruits in the world.

Apples are favored for many reasons. They can be eaten fresh, whether whole, sliced, or diced.

They can be baked, roasted, stewed, boiled, or converted into juices, sauces, spreads, or jellies, whether as part of a main meal or dessert. If stored in a cool, dry place, they will also keep for weeks or months, providing refreshment and nutrition long after harvest time. They can also be dried, canned, and preserved to last even longer than that. Apples are simply delicious and refreshing, keeping their flavor and texture in many different kinds of dishes.

Another old saying is "an apple a day keeps the doctor away." That is partly because apples are sources of not only sweet-tasting energy but also vitamins, minerals, and fiber. This was especially important in earlier times, before modern storage, because during the winter people had few other fresh fruits and vegetables available.

Beyond all else, apple trees are also beautiful. Some varieties are, in fact, grown as ornamental trees for that reason, especially the crab apple. In China and Japan some dwarf apple trees are even grown in flower pots for their beautiful pink blossoms and red fruits.

Red, green, or any color in between, an apple is always a tasty treat. In early North America and right up into the mid-1900s, a shiny apple was often given as a gift to a teacher or special friend. Apples are still tucked into many lunchboxes.

The apple grows from a blossom at the end of a twig, and its stem sometimes has a leaf or two attached to it, as here. Inside the tasty outer part is the core that we don't eat, which contains tough tissue surrounding the seeds.

What Are Apples?

The apple and the rose are cousins. Both belong to the very large *Rosa* family, which also includes many other fruits, such as the pear, cherry, plum, peach, strawberry, raspberry, nectarine, apricot, quince, and even the almond!

The apple itself is the fruit of the apple tree (known to biologists as *Malus*). Its shiny, tough skin covers its tasty "flesh," which encloses several seeds. New trees can grow from these seeds, though apple trees today are usually started from other apple trees (see p. 19).

Starting Life

Each apple begins with a flower. In the spring, after a wintertime of sleeping (see p. 17), the apple tree puts out many sweet-smelling blossoms. Deep pink on the outside and pale pink shading to white on the inside when opened, these blossoms are one of the loveliest signs of spring. Apple growers call the time of their arrival simply "the pink."

At the bottom of each blossom is a round organ called the *ovary*. Inside the ovary are smaller organs called *ovules*. If all goes well, the ovules will become the seeds of the apple and the ovary will become the fleshy part that we love to eat.

For that to happen, the ovary must be *pollinated*—that is, it must receive some of a dustlike material called *pollen* that develops at the top

(Left) Apples begin with blossoms. The outer side of the closed blossom is often deep pink, but the inner side of the open blossom is usually a very pale pink tinged with the deeper color. Inside and unseen is the ovary, which becomes the apple. (Below) Honeybees go from tree to tree seeking sweet nectar from flowers like this apple blossom. In the process they transfer pollen from one blossom to another. This pollination is necessary for the apple fruits to develop and grow properly.

of stalks in the flower's center. Most varieties of apple must receive pollen from other apple trees (sometimes from other varieties), not from their own flowers—that is, they must be *cross-pollinated*. That is why apple trees grow best in *orchards*, fields containing many such trees.

Pollination of apple trees is mainly carried out by honeybees. Like most flowers, apple blossoms produce a sweet liquid called *nectar*, which attracts honeybees. When bees come to drink the nectar, their bodies brush against the blossom's pollen-producing stalks, picking up some of the pollen. As the bees move to other blossoms, they pick up some new pollen and brush off some old, so pollen from one flower ends up in another.

Pollination is so important that many apple growers bring in honeybees for that purpose. The bees live in specially built boxlike hives. In the springtime beekeepers load the hives onto trucks and take them from farm to farm to pollinate apple trees (and many other crops). In the process bees gather nectar and take it back to the hives, where they convert it into honey.

The Apple Grows

After pollination the ovary begins to grow. This is called *fruitset*. The petals and most other parts of the flower either drop away or become part of the fruit. The ovary's outer layer becomes the thin, shiny, protective skin of the apple. The ovules become seeds, normally two each enclosed in five small, tough compartments in the core, the part of the apple we do not eat. The rest of the ovary develops into the tasty flesh of the apple.

The apple tree draws in water and nutrients (nourishing substances) through its roots in the ground. During the growing season its green leaves use sunlight, carbon dioxide (a common gas) from the air, and water to make various sugars, in a process called *photosynthesis*.

The sweet-tasting sugars are car-

These are young apples—actually swelling ovaries—after what biologists call *fruitset*. Some of the leaves have browned because of fire blight, one of the dozens of diseases and pests that can threaten growing apples.

Apples do not ripen and grow all at once. Especially if temperatures are sharply variable, swinging between warm and cold, early blossoms can be pollinated and grow to full size, while some blossoms are just setting fruit and still others are just opening. That is what has happened with this Braeburn apple tree, which has fully grown apples, just-set fruits (bottom left), and fresh blossoms on a single branch.

bohydrates, energy-supplying substances made of the elements (basic substances) carbon, hydrogen, and oxygen. These sugars fuel the growth of the tree itself and also its fruits. As the apple grows, some of these sugars are stored in the form of *starch* within the fleshy fruits.

Apples grow to different sizes, depending on the variety. When it reaches its full size, a thin layer of cells (the *abscission layer*) forms near the base of the stem. This gradually hardens and cuts off the supply of water and nutrients to the apple. At this point the apple is on its own and is said to be *mature*.

However, it is not yet ripe. During ripening, various changes take place that give the apple its look, smell, and taste. Much of the starch is converted back into sugars.

After picking, apples are put in large bins like these. This crew boss in a Maine orchard is checking a bin of just-picked McIntosh apples. They will then be quickly moved into cold storage for longer keeping.

At the same time the flesh of the apple becomes softer.

During ripening, the apple also turns its final color. Most ripe apples are some shade of red, occasionally yellow or orange. A few varieties are green, but green apples, such as the Granny Smith, have only recently been widely accepted.

Mature, ripe apples vary in size and shape, depending on the variety. They are generally round, though some are more oval. They usually have indentations at each end, one

where the stem joins the twig, the other where the flower once was. They are generally two to six inches across and can weigh anything from a few ounces to more than a pound, depending on the variety.

Mature apples can be picked some days or even weeks before they are fully ripe (see p. 23). They can then ripen in storage, as is done with most commercially grown apples today. Kept in cool, dark places, apples will keep for weeks or months (some varieties better than others)—but only if they are undamaged. If the skin is broken or bruised, the flesh will quickly discolor or spoil.

Modern scientists have developed even better ways to store apples, using *controlled-atmosphere storage*. Kept at cool temperatures, with less oxygen and more carbon dioxide or other gases than in outside air, some varieties of apples can last for a year or even more. As a result people can now have fresh apples the whole year round.

Fresh, ripe apples are almost 84 percent water, which is one reason they are so refreshing to eat. They are almost 15 percent carbohy-drates, primarily the sugars *glucose*, *fructose*, and *sucrose*. They also contain vitamins A and C and small amounts of calcium, iron, magnesium, and potassium, primarily concentrated in the skin, but very little fat, protein, or other nutrients. Their main flavors come from compounds called *volatiles* and various acids, primarily *malic acid*.

If apples are not picked, they eventually drop to the ground. Then the flesh of the apple is eaten by animals or rots away, leaving seeds that might grow into new trees.

Some kinds of apples, such as crab apples and wild apples, can be very small, but others can be enormous. This one apple alone weighs almost three pounds!

The Apple's Journey

Braeburn

Cameo

Gala

Golden Delicious

Cortland

People have been gathering and eating apples for thousands of years. We know this because archaeologists have found remains of apples at many prehistoric dwelling sites.

However, the apples known in early Europe and Asia are not the kind we eat today. Instead, they were small, sour-tasting apples, probably much like the fruits of crab apple trees that still grow wild in many parts of Europe and Asia.

Shaping Modern Apples

The large, sweet-tasting apples we know today were shaped by humans. They probably started with various kinds of wild crab apple trees that grew in eastern Europe and western Asia, especially around the Caspian Sea, in what are now southern Russia and Kazakhstan.

More than 10,000 years ago humans learned how to cultivate plants—that is, deliberately grow and harvest them. Early farmers quickly began to shape plants by choosing the seeds of the largest and most attractive plants for growing the next year's crop.

However, apple trees are unlike many other plants. When you grow apple trees from seeds, the resulting fruits are different from the original apples. Sometimes the apples are larger and tastier. Indeed, many of today's most popular varieties originated by chance from seedlings. However, apples from seed-grown trees are more often smaller and less tasty.

If an apple tree has large, tasty apples, the only way to grow more of the same kind of apples is by grafting (see p. 19). Grafting techniques were being applied to apple trees in

Granny Smith

McIntosh

Jonagold

Red Delicious

Fuji

Rome Beauty

the Mediterranean regions of Europe and Asia by at least 900 B.C.

By the 500s B.C., in the great age of Greek civilization, the techniques of grafting apple trees were well developed. They were developed even further by the Romans. Writing in the first century A.D., the Roman writer Pliny described grafting in great detail and listed some two dozen varieties of apples (though many may have been other fruits; see p. 16). Archaeologists have even found remains of apple trees preserved in the ruins of Pompeii, a Roman city buried by lava from the Mt. Vesuvius volcano in 79 A.D.

Such apple trees, shaped by humans, have spread around the world. By Roman times they were grown widely across Europe and in those parts of western and central Asia where the climate was right (see p. 17). However, they did not reach China until the Middle Ages.

After the fall of the Roman Empire, knowledge of some grafting techniques (like much other knowledge) was lost in Europe. However, much survived in the Muslim world, and centuries later the techniques were reintroduced into Europe.

By the 1600s the French had developed techniques of pruning, grafting to get dwarf trees, and training branches. These would be adopted by modern apple growers in high-density orchards (see p. 21).

Spreading around the World

Before the arrival of Europeans, only crab apples grew in the Americas. English colonists settling in Massachu-

These are fruits on a modern crab apple tree. Our modern apple is believed to have been developed from trees with small fruits like these. Apple trees are prey to many diseases, such as the apple scab that has caused browning of the leaves on this tree.

setts introduced the apple tree to New England in the 1620s. The trees soon became well established there, for the climate was ideal for them. Apples were quickly adopted by the Iroquois, who lived in northeastern North America.

Apples spread even more widely in North America during the early 1800s. A wandering Massachusetts-born preacher named John Chapman gathered seeds from a Pennsylvania cider mill and headed westward down the Ohio River and out as far as Indiana. Along the way he planted apple seeds, establishing many new orchards. His work gave him a popular nickname: Johnny Appleseed.

Many of the resulting apples were small and sour-tasting, like the fruits of many apple trees grown from seeds. However, they were

The modern apple, believed to have been developed from crab apples in west-central Eurasia, is grown widely throughout Eurasia. These apples are being sorted and packed in Kashmir, a region disputed by India and Pakistan.

good for cider, dried apples, and animal feed. More important, some of the resulting apples were very tasty, indeed. These formed the basis for new American varieties of apples, such as the Northern Spy, the Jonathan, and the Red Delicious.

Apples reached the Pacific Northwest with settlers in the 1840s. Henderson Llewelling brought apple trees (and other plants) by covered wagon to the Willamette Valley in Oregon in 1845. In the process he helped found what would become an enormous apple industry in western North America.

Meanwhile European colonists also spread apples elsewhere around the world to places such as Australia, New Zealand, Argentina, and South Africa. These regions also developed their own special varieties of apples, such as the Granny Smith, discovered in Australia in 1868.

Adam and Eve were forced to leave the Garden of Eden because they ate "the fruit of the tree of knowledge of good and evil." Since the Middle Ages many people have thought that fruit was an apple, as shown in this American folk art painting.

Was It an Apple?

What fruit did Adam and Eve eat in the Garden of Eden? We do not know. The early Hebrew texts of the biblical story simply say they ate the "fruit of the tree of knowledge of good and evil." The tradition that this fruit was an apple dates back only to about the 400s A.D. Europeans translating the Bible took the fruit to be the apple, probably because that was the most widely grown and eaten fruit they knew.

Another famous apple-related phrase from the Bible is Solomon's "Comfort me with apples." However, many modern biologists think that the original text probably referred to a quince or possibly an apricot.

One of the most beautiful sights of spring is an apple orchard in bloom. The blossoms open around the same time as many early wildflowers.

Growing Apples

Apple trees can grow in many parts of the world. However, they grow best in places with moderate rainfall and temperatures.

If the weather is too cold for too long, as in northern Canada, the tree can be killed. If it is too hot for too long, as in a southern Florida summer, the tree may grow, but it will not flower or produce fruit well. Too much water at one time or overall can also affect the fruit.

To put out fruit properly, an apple tree needs a period of cool to cold weather—about 900 or 1,000 hours (39–42 days) with temperatures of less than 45 degrees Fahrenheit. This puts the tree into *dormancy* (sleep).

In the springtime warmer temperatures and longer days trigger the apple tree to end its "sleep." Then it begins to put out leaf buds and flowers, beginning the cycle that will result in tasty fruits (see p.

6). Without that sleeping period to trigger the cycle, the tree may produce no apples or only a few.

As a result apple trees grow best in regions of *temperate* (moderate) climate. These include much of the United States, Europe, Australia, and New Zealand, and those parts of Asia, Africa, and South America where the climate is suitable.

Today Russia and the countries of the former Soviet Union together produce by far the largest amount of apples. The United States is second, followed by China, France, Italy, Germany, Poland, Turkey, and Hungary. Within the United States by far the leading apple-producing state is Washington, followed by New York, Michigan, California, Pennsylvania, Virginia, North Carolina, and West Virginia.

Even within suitable growing areas, apple fruits are sensitive to extremes. A late frost after a tree has started budding and flowering can stunt fruit growth. So can a dry summer or a long period of drenching rains.

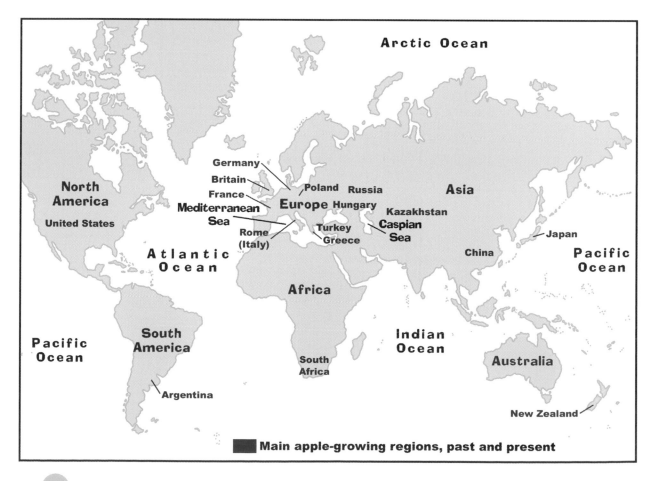

Main apple-growing regions, past and present

The most popular apple variety in the world and the second most popular apple in the United States is the Golden Delicious. The only variety more popular in the United States is its "cousin," the Red Delicious.

Leading Varieties

Some varieties of apples are best suited for particular climates. The McIntosh apple grows best in New England, for example, where its color and flavor are enhanced by the cool nights. However, the York Imperial is better suited to northern Virginia, with its longer growing season. In Russia the leading variety is the Antonovka, which can survive colder winters than many other varieties.

Several thousand varieties of apples are recognized, but only a few dozen are grown commercially in large numbers. The most widely grown apple in the world is the Golden Delicious, second-favorite in the United States but the top apple in mainland Europe. Second in the world, but first in the United States, is the Red Delicious. Third in the world, but by far the leader in Britain, is Cox's Orange Pippen. Following those in order of popularity are the Rome Beauty, Belle de Boskop, Granny Smith, Jonathan, and McIntosh varieties.

Starting Orchards

The seeds found in the core of an apple can be used to grow apple trees. However, the resulting apples

New apple trees are generally grown from branches or buds of trees grafted onto a rootstock, a tree with an existing root system. Here branches (*scions*) are being attached to the trunk of a rootstock apple tree in early spring.

look and taste quite different from the apple the seeds came from (see p. 12).

Because of that, most apple trees are started from other apple trees, not from seeds. Growers choose a tree with desirable apples and cut off buds or branches (called *scions*). They then *graft* (attach) these onto a *rootstock*, a tree with an already well-established root system. If the graft is successful, the two grow together as one tree.

Grafting is a form of *cloning*, and most apples of a particular variety are *clones* of each other. This means that their genes—the basic set of biological codes that guide the fruit's growth and development— are identical.

Many rootstock trees are grown from vigorous seedlings raised in protective nurseries, though some are older, well-established trees. When a rootstock seedling is about 18 months old, growers will graft the bud or branch onto it. The grafted tree often remains in a nursery for another year or two before being planted outside in an orchard.

Another six to eight years may pass before the tree begins to produce significant quantities of apples. However, if the trees remain healthy, they will continue to produce for decades (though not every year in some varieties).

During the life of the tree the grower must carefully watch over its health, training it to grow as desired and protecting it from pests, disease, and severe weather. To fight pests and disease, many growers use chemicals called *pesticides*.

However, many people are concerned about environmental damage from pesticide use. Scientists are working to develop apple varieties that naturally resist disease and pests.

Traditional and Modern

A spreading apple tree is a beautiful sight, whether in springtime when full of blossoms or in autumn when full of fruit. If left to them-

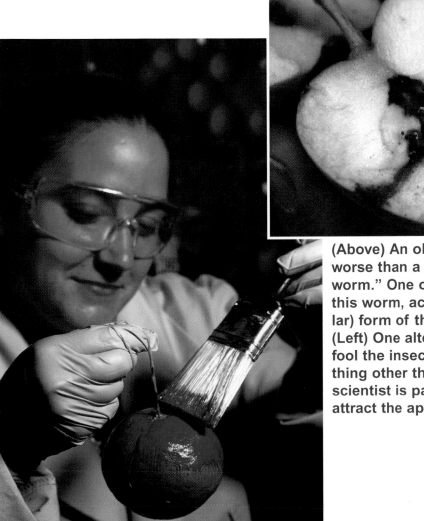

(Above) An old joke goes "What's worse than a worm in an apple? Half a worm." One of the worst apple pests is this worm, actually the larva (caterpillar) form of the codling moth.
(Left) One alternative to pesticides is to fool the insects into attacking something other than the real apple. This scientist is painting a decoy to try to attract the apple maggot fly.

selves, apple trees grow to about 30 to 35 feet tall, with a high, rounded crown. Traditional apple orchards tend to have large trees in widely spaced rows.

The problem with spreading trees is that the leaves on the lower branches often do not get enough sun, so those branches often have fewer or smaller apples. As a result growers have for many centuries pruned (cut away) some branches, so the remaining ones can get more sun.

Modern apple growers have adopted some new approaches to old problems, including several techniques developed by the French (see p. 13). The result is that newly established apple orchards are quite different from traditional ones.

Modern growers tend to prune far more aggressively. The remaining branches are often tied to posts or wires to make sure that every branch gets enough sun.

Modern growers also tend to use dwarf (6 to 8 feet tall) or semidwarf (9 to 15 feet tall) rootstocks. Though fed by a large root system, these dwarf varieties are much smaller above the ground, often with just a few branches. The result is that the

These are dwarf apple trees growing Jonagold apples in the state of Washington. Dwarf tree branches often need support, especially when heavy with fruit, as here.

trees produce more fruits per branch.

In addition, the smaller trees can be placed closer together. This means that a plot of land can carry more dwarf trees than a traditional orchard. Such orchards of highly pruned and trained dwarf trees are called *high-density orchards*, and the practices used are called *intensive cultivation*.

Harvesting Apples

Modern or traditional, apples still must be harvested. When apples are ripe (see p. 10), you can simply twist one at the stem, and it will come off right in your hand. And that is how most apples are still harvested—by hand.

In traditional apple orchards people usually stand on ladders to reach the high branches. In orchards of dwarf trees people can often pick the apples while standing on the ground.

Harvesters must be careful not to bruise or cut the skin because that lessens the value of the apple. Damaged apples cannot be sold in stores, and they are less good for processing. They can be used for cider but only if used right away.

Tree-shaking machines exist, some with cushioned catching areas, but most kinds of apples are too readily damaged for this kind of harvesting.

Harvested apples are placed in large bins and quickly shipped either to storage facilities (see p. 11) or to processing plants (see p. 27).

Unlike most food crops today, apples are still generally picked the old-fashioned way—by hand.

In North America cider normally refers to the fresh-squeezed, unprocessed juice of the apple, often served warm with a cinnamon stick as here. The flesh of the apple can also be converted into a spread called apple butter, as on this bread.

The Many Uses of Apples

From the start apples have been enjoyed fresh, either just after picking or from cold storage. However, apples are used in many other ways. In the United States nearly half of the annual apple crop is sent to factories for processing into apple-based products. These offer variety and also extend the use of apples as food beyond their life in storage.

One of the oldest ways of processing apples, going back thousands of years, is to dry them. Dried apples have been found in Mesopotamia (what is now Iraq) dating back to before 2000 B.C. The tradition has continued into modern times.

Apples for drying first must be peeled and their cores removed. Then they are sliced into thin sec-

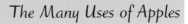

tions and dried in the sun or heat (or today freeze-dried). Dried apples can be a tasty and nutritious food months after harvest time. In colonial America people often held *apple bees*, parties where they would talk and sing together while peeling and coring apples for drying.

Juice and Cider

Making juice is also a very old use for apples. Juice squeezed out of apples makes cider. For many centuries cider was made by hand, using small farm presses, but today it is often made in large factories. Either way, the process is basically the same.

First sorters inspect the apples and remove those unsuitable for use. Then the apples are washed and ground into a mash—skin, seeds, and all.

In traditional cidermaking the mash is wrapped in a heavy cloth in a flat form to make what is called a *cheese*. A number of cheeses are stacked inside the cider press. Then the machine presses down on them, forcing juice out of the mash. The

This is an old-fashioned cider press being used to squeeze juice out of apples. The press squeezes several *cheeses* (layers) at a time. This juice, being squeezed in France's Normandy region, will become an apple brandy called Calvados.

leftover solid matter, called *pomace*, can be fed to animals or spread to enrich soil.

In modern factories large automated presses press the mash, with one worker tending several machines. These do not use cloth-wrapped cheeses. Instead sterilized rice hulls or other material may be added to the mash before pressing.

Either way the resulting liquid is fresh cider. This has tiny flecks of apple floating in it, giving it a brownish color. This liquid can be treated in various ways to remove

many of the bits, producing a clear apple juice. In the United States about one quarter of the yearly apple crop is converted into juice or cider. This can be packaged and sold fresh or, after water has been removed, as a frozen concentrate.

If held for a time, especially unrefrigerated, cider will begin to "turn" or ferment. Cidermakers can control this process, which turns the cider into an alcoholic drink that Americans call *hard cider* and Europeans call simply *cider*.

Further processes can turn hard

On arrival at a processing plant, apples are first sorted and any damaged fruits or unwanted matter are removed. That's what workers are doing as this apple-covered conveyor belt moves by them.

Applesauce is a favorite American dish, not much eaten elsewhere in the world. Some is made at home, but most is made in factories, often from a mixture of different varieties of apples, to get the most desirable texture, flavor, and color.

cider into more concentrated alcoholic drinks, such as wine or brandy (in America sometimes called *applejack*). The most famous apple brandy, often aged in huge wooden barrels, is *Calvados*, named for its homeland in France's Normandy region. Cider can also be turned into vinegar, which is used in cooking.

Processing Apples

Apples are also processed to make many other kinds of products. First the skin and cores are removed (and sometimes pressed for their remaining juices). If you make an apple pie or applesauce from scratch, you have to peel and core the apples by hand, the traditional way. However, machines do those jobs in modern factories.

Some are mechanical, spinning the apple around coring and peeling blades. Some use steam in pressurized chambers to remove the skins, though that causes a brown ring to form on the fruit and creates wastewater for disposal. Some use chemicals to remove skins, after which the apples are washed. Apples peeled by steam or chemicals are then cored by other machines.

What happens next depends on the final product. In the United

When first created at New York City's Waldorf Hotel in the 1890s, Waldorf salad contained only a mixture of apples (sprinkled with lemon juice) and chopped celery mixed with mayonnaise and served on a bed of lettuce. Today it generally also includes walnuts, as here.

States (but much less elsewhere in the world) a favorite product is applesauce. Apples are cut into small pieces and then seasoned and cooked until the pieces are very soft. The resulting applesauce is then passed through a sieve (a wire mesh strainer), to remove any remaining unwanted bits, such as seeds. Applesauce is often made of a mixture of different kinds of apples, to give the desired color, texture, and taste.

The other main factory product is sliced apples. Most apples begin to turn slightly brown as soon as the skin is cut open. To prevent that, sliced apples are often put briefly into a slightly salty solution. After further sorting, inspection, and trimming, many are immediately packed into steel cans. Others may be frozen or freeze-dried for later use. Most eventually end up in apple pies.

In the United States about one quarter of the entire yearly apple crop goes to commercially canned applesauce and apple slices. Some kinds of apples can be sold for either eating fresh or processing, depending on market conditions at harvest time. These include the Golden Delicious, Rome Beauty,

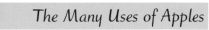

Jonathan, Stayman Winesap, Cortland, Yellow Newtown, McIntosh, and Idared varieties.

However, some apple varieties are grown primarily for commercial processing and are seldom sold fresh. For example, the very soft Twenty Ounce apple is used primarily for babies' applesauce.

Apples are also used in many other ways. They may end up in jellies and marmalades. They may be converted into candied apple rings, a popular garnish on dinner plates. Applesauce and fresh cider can also be concentrated to form a creamy spread called *apple butter*.

Many apples are bought for home cooking. Besides pies, a favorite dessert is baked apples, in which the cored (but not peeled) fruits are filled with sugar and spices and baked. Some can also be peeled and then wrapped in dough to make apple tarts. Apples are even used in salads, such as the Waldorf salad, and as part of many main dishes around the world. The varieties are endless—and are a key to the popularity of the apple.

In making an apple tart, the cores are removed from peeled apples and the empty spaces are filled with nuts, raisins, and various seasonings. The apples are then wrapped in a rolled dough, as here in unbaked tarts (top left) and a baked one (bottom left).

Words to Know

carbohydrates Chemical compounds (mixed substances) made of the elements (basic substances) carbon, hydrogen, and oxygen, in apples mostly the sugars *glucose*, *fructose*, and *sucrose*.

cheese In traditional cidermaking a flat layer of mashed apples, wrapped in cloth. Several cheeses are stacked and squeezed to produce the apple's juices.

clones: See GRAFTING; GENES.

controlled-atmosphere storage Cool conditions with less oxygen and more carbon dioxide or other gases, which allow some apples to last for a year or more.

crab apples Apple trees that bear small, sour-tasting fruits. Early wild apple trees were probably much like these.

cross-pollination: See POLLINATION.

dormancy A cool "sleeping" period of about 40 days required for apple trees to produce fruits well.

dwarf trees Trees smaller than traditional apple trees, generally only 6 to 8 feet tall. Trees 9 to 15 feet tall are called *semidwarf*.

fructose: See CARBOHYDRATES.

fruitset The normal growth of an OVARY after POLLINATION, the beginning of the apple fruit.

genes The basic set of biological codes that guide growth and development. Clones have identical genes (see GRAFTING).

glucose: See CARBOHYDRATES.

grafting The technique of attaching a branch (*scion*) or bud from one tree onto the ROOTSTOCK of another. Grafting is a form of *cloning*, which means that the GENES of the new apples are the same as those of the original apples. Apples of the same variety are *clones* of one another.

high-density orchard Orchards of heavily pruned (see PRUNING) and trained DWARF trees placed close together, allowing more apples to be produced from a section of land. These practices are called *intensive cultivation*.

intensive cultivation: See HIGH-DENSITY ORCHARD.

malic acid A substance that helps give apples their taste.

Malus A biological name for apples.

mature Describing an apple that has grown to full size but is not yet RIPE. At maturity water and nutrients from the tree are cut off.

nectar A sweet-smelling liquid produced by apple blossoms (and many other flowers). It attracts honeybees, which help with POLLINATION.

orchard Fields containing many fruit trees, useful for POLLINATION.

ovary A small round structure deep inside an apple blossom. If pollinated, it grows into the apple fruit (see POLLINATION).

ovules Small structures inside the OVARY of an apple blossom flower. If the ovary is pollinated (see POLLINATION), the ovules grow into apple seeds, from which new apple trees can grow.

pesticides Chemicals used to fight pests and diseases that can attack a plant and damage or destroy its fruits.

photosynthesis The process by which plants use sunlight, carbon dioxide, and water to make CARBOHYDRATES.

pollination The process of transferring the dust-like material called *pollen* from the top of a flower to the OVARY in the bottom. Most apple trees need to receive pollen from other apple trees (sometimes other varieties); they are described as *cross-pollinated*.

pomace The solid matter left over after juice has been squeezed from apples, as in making cider.

pruning Cutting away some branches to let the rest of the tree grow and produce fruits better.

ripe A MATURE apple that has undergone other changes, including changing color, softening, and converting STARCH back to sugars.

rootstock The lower part of a tree with its root system, today often DWARF TREES, to which branches (*scions*) or buds of other trees are attached (see GRAFTING).

Rosa The rose family of plants, to which apples and many other fruits belong.

scions: See ROOTSTOCK; GRAFTING.

semidwarf: See DWARF TREES.

starch The form in which sugars (see CARBOHYDRATES) are stored while an apple is growing.

sucrose: See CARBOHYDRATES.

temperate climate Moderate temperatures and rainfall, the type of climate preferred by apple trees.

volatiles Substances that help give apples their taste.

On the Internet

The Internet has many interesting sites about apples. The site addresses often change, so the best way to find current addresses is to go to a search site, such as www.yahoo.com. Type in a word or phrase, such as "apples."

As this book was being written, websites about apples included:

http://www.usapple.org/
U.S. Apple Association website, offering information for students, teachers, consumers, and others, also including images, recipes, and more.

http://www.appleproducts.org/
Processed Apples Institute website, offering information on harvesting and processing, plus recipes, nutritional data, and more.

http://www.urbanext.uiuc.edu/apples/
Apples & More, a website of the University of Illinois extension, with facts, figures, recipes, history, and more information.

http://www.norfolk-county.com/bigapple/cider.htm
The Big Apple Cider Company site, showing how cider is made.

In Print

Your local library system will have various books on apples. The following is just a sampling of them.

Barritt, Bruce H., with K. Bert van Dalfsin. *Intensive Orchard Management: A Practical Guide to the Planning, Establishment and Management of High Density Apple Orchards*. Yakima, WA: Good Fruit Grower, 1992.

Browning, Frank. *Apples*. New York: North Point Press, 1998.

Manhart, Warren. *Apples for the Twenty-First Century*. Portland, OR: North American Tree Co., 1995.

O'Rourke, A. Desmond. *The World Apple Market*. New York: Food Products Press/Haworth Press, 1994.

Phillips, Michael. *The Apple Grower: A Guide for the Organic Orchardist*. White River Junction, VT: Chelsea Green, 1998.

Processed Apple Products. Donald L. Downing, ed. New York: Van Nostrand Reinhold, 1989.

Rosenstein, Mark. *In Praise of Apples: A Harvest of History, Horticulture and Recipes*. Asheville, NC: Lark Books, 1996.

Van Nostrand's Scientific Encyclopedia, 8th ed., 2 vols. Douglas M. Considine and Glenn D. Considine, eds. New York: Van Nostrand Reinhold, 1995.

Yepsen, Roger B. *Apples*. New York: Norton, 1994.

Apples

Index